WOMEN·at·WAR

Liverpool Women 1939-45

p a t · a y e r s

L I V E R · P

Illustrations acknowledgements

Sincere thanks to the following for permission to reproduce illustrations:

City Engineers Department, Liverpool - 1

Liverpool City Libraries - 2, 3, 6

National Museums and Galleries on Merseyside - 8

Alex Grant - frontispiece, 4, 7, 10

Mrs. L. Ayers (born Harrison) - 5

Mrs. K. Harkins (born May) - 8

First published 1988 by Liver Press, 1 & 3 Grove Road, Rock Ferry, Birkenhead, Wirral, Merseyside L42 3XS.

Copyright © Pat Ayers, 1988.
Printed by Birkenhead Press Limited, 1 & 3 Grove Road, Rock Ferry, Birkenhead, Merseyside L42 3XS.

ISBN 1 871201 00 4

· CONTENTS ·

For my mother
Rose Mason (born Kirwan)
with love.

Preface

When War was declared in September 1939, the people of Britain entered a period which was to leave few lives untouched. In Liverpool, almost overnight, war brought changes to all aspects of day-to-day living. In particular, war had an immediate effect on the lives of women. It is the impact of war on Liverpool women which provides the focus for this study.

The original research for this work was done in the Summer and Autumn of 1980. In the time since, there has been increasing interest in women's history at all levels, which has given expression to the feeling that history taught in schools, colleges and universities has not adequately reflected women's experiences. Throughout Liverpool, valuable research by individual women and women working together in history groups, is doing much to redress the balance. This work is making our foremother's visible and giving value and recognition to the contribution they have made across all periods and cultures thus uniting younger and older women with bonds of shared experience.

It would be impossible for me to acknowledge individually all those people who have given me help during my research; to you all many thanks. Dorothy Wainright of the Mass Observation Archive, Linda Grant and Penny Summerfield freely extended their courtesy, help and interest during my initial research. I am grateful to Pat Hudson for her kindness, constructive advice and enduring patience, and to my dear friends Linda Pepper, Marij Van Helmond, Edith Hamilton, Sheila Wood and Jan Lambertz for their continued love and support. Many thanks also to Paula McConville, Kevin Moore and Alan Johnson my co-workers at Docklands History Project, University of Liverpool. As always, Janet Smith of Liverpool City Record Office has given freely of her knowledge. Loraine Knowles, Gordon Read and Val Burton of National Museums and Galleries on Merseyside, have been unfailing in their responsive courtesy and very valuable assistance. Many, many thanks to Susan Yee and Ian Qualtrough of the Photographic Unit at Liverpool University for all the work they have done for me and also to Val Taylor for typesetting. I am particularly grateful to Andy Bone and Maggie Bayley for a very thoughtfully designed and illustrated cover.

Most especially, I shall always be in the debt of the many Liverpool people who shared their memories of the war years with me. In particular, Mrs. F. Henshaw of Old Swan who sadly died before the book was published and Mrs. L. Ayers, Mrs. E. York, Miss Nevin and Mr. J. Kinsella.

Women workers photographed at Kirkby Munitions Factory.

The Phoney War

An Old Timer's Growl

There's lipstick on the drinking cups,
There's talcum on the bench,
There's cold cream on the surface plate,
Hand lotion on the wrench,
And 'Soir de Paris' scents the air,
That once held lube oil's smell—
I've just picked up a curling pin,
Believe me—War is hell![1]

By the time the above was reproduced in a local work's magazine in 1944, women were very firmly established as an integral part of the paid workforce of the country. However, although the Government had gone to the vast expense of compiling registers of women who might be called upon to work, the large- scale absorption of women into industry was not initially envisaged. Despite the lessons of the First World War the potential of women's labour was largely ignored. It is clear that the Chamberlain Government did not foresee the mobilisation of women in industry on any scale; it was concerned for women to carry on as usual. A Bulletin of Information issued on 5 September 1939, urged women not to leave their current employment in commerce and industry:

'The life of the nation must go on and it will make for confusion if large numbers of women seek to change their jobs. The woman who remains at work and volunteers in her spare time for a part-time service which still needs recruits is doing her full part in national service.'[2]

Not all women, however, were able to 'carry on as usual'. Indeed, in the beginning, unemployment among women increased and remained high until February 1941.[3] To a certain extent this was unavoidable, normal trading was dislocated, evacuation was disruptive and cinemas and theatres closed. Mrs. T. worked as a cleaner in a local cinema:

> '. . . I was shocked. Even though people'd been talking about it for weeks, you always think things won't actually happen. There was so much to think about with the kids and that . . . then the Manager of the picture house sent his lad up to say that I wasn't to go in because he had orders not to open up. I tell you that was as big a shock (laughing) if not bigger—I relied on it.'[4]

But lack of activity on the industrial front was in sharp contrast to the frantic Air Raid Protection (ARP) plans made in an attempt to lessen the expected holocaust, panic and social disorder following on from aerial bombardment. It was thought unwise to allow people to assemble in large public shelters so the Anderson Shelter, together with the strengthening of basement and ground floor rooms, was made the primary form of ARP. Every member of the population was issued with a gas mask and these quickly became part and parcel of wartime life. In addition, the Government believed that there would be a mass exodus from the industrial areas so in an effort to control it a programme of evacuation was developed.

A sense of desperation hung over all plans. The authorities were anxious to get the 'helpless' away before the expected bombs began to fall. Although those eligible had been registered earlier in the school holidays, the outbreak of war came sooner than anticipated. In Liverpool, Government instructions were received a few minutes before noon on 31 August and were at once circulated to all schools. 226 special trains left Liverpool between Friday 1 September and Wednesday 6th.[5]

The journeys of the evacuees were often long and distressing because of the inadequate water supply and the absence of lavatories, especially when journeys were so much longer than usual. A Liverpool school teacher superintended a party of children on '. . . a corridor train which stank' and which took twelve hours to reach its destination.[6] Even less fortunate were those on a non-corridor train which carried 400 mothers and children under five to Pwllheli.[7]

2

No. 1 *Liverpool children reading evacuation instructions in their school playground.*

The actual experience of evacuation devastated much of the country. Evacuation followed a long period of widespread unemployment, and living conditions for much of the population of Liverpool were appalling in terms of poverty and material deprivation. In general, it was those areas of most decay, situated as they were in the city centre or along the docksides, that were considered to be in most danger of air attack and the inhabitants of which were most in need of transference to places of safety. The people of the receiving areas, who knew nothing of urban conditions were shocked when confronted with them. There was an almost complete lack of understanding of the sort of situation many of the evacuees had come from and widespread criticism of the parents of children who had been sent to live away 'inadequately dressed'. Liverpool became known as the 'Plimsoll City'. However, children were generally sent away in the best their parents could afford. As one Liverpool schoolteacher, evacuated with her school to Sandbach, recalled:

'... I think probably the biggest problem came over clothing

3

because if you've only got a back yard in which three or four families dry their clothes, your clothes never looked snow white...they (the receiving families) thought they were all dirty and took them off and went out and bought them new which was rather sad for kids because probably mother had taken great care to get their clothes together and patched it all up.'[8]

In Liverpool, there was some appreciation of the difficulties some mothers faced:

'...I remember Lewis's sending a van full up of baby clothes and saying, 'Will you push it in wherever the children need clothing?' We had a mad rush on...and we were pushing in things for children who hadn't got very much.'[9]

One mother had had to send one roller towel for six children: '...we had to cut it up into five or six pieces so that every child had a bit of towelling to go with him or her; it was nothing more than a face cloth really, just a strip.'[10] Apart from the actual appearance of the evacuees, there was even greater shocked outrage, when it was discovered that many of them were verminous and/or diseased. The Medical Officer of Health for Liverpool received widespread criticism for allowing them to leave the city in such a condition and without doubt, many of the Liverpool children were in a poor state.[11] Evacuation, coming as it did at the end of the summer holidays, meant the children had not been under the eye of the school medical service before they left the city. Also, the conditions of the journey to the reception areas meant that vermin, like lice, were easily transferred from child to child.

Less measurable, but if anything even more inflamatory, were the social habits of many evacuees. Foster-parents were horrified to find many of Liverpool's little girls had never worn knickers and a large percentage had never possessed pyjamas. But in the conditions of poverty many children came from, underwear and sleep attire were hardly priorities. As another evacuated schoolteacher remembered: '...the foster-parents expected them to have nighties on, but of course they didn't, they just took off the top layer and got into bed!'[12] Bed-wetting was a major problem, although not perhaps to be unexpected given the emotional upheaval.

On top of the lack of understanding of the dreadful conditions that many dockland working-class children came from, black children carried the additional burden of racism. This was not, however, a product of evacuation, as shown in the notes of one Liverpool schoolteacher who recorded for Mass Observation: 'Felt sorry for the receiving area or district—the mothers are a mixed crowd—black, white, yellow in various degrees, dirty, immoral and quarrelsome and drinking. Pity the poor billeting officer.'[13] Many of those who lived in the receiving areas had never seen black people before; this didn't prevent many from making arbitrary judgements about their suitability for accommodation:

> '...They were the children that they had difficulty in billeting...particularly if you had 'mixed' parentage, the people...even the 'knowledgeable' ones in the council offices, took one look at the children and decided they couldn't go with their natural brothers and sisters...The children were looked upon ascance and their mothers weren't welcome because they thought they had four fathers for four children.'[14]

For all children the experience was potentially traumatic. Parental visiting was generally discouraged and in any case, the costs involved were often prohibitive and increased the isolation of children sent away. In instances where mothers accompanied their children, the clash of cultures was often even greater and led to much distress on both sides. The main problem was a complete lack of comprehension, by both the evacuees and the billeting families, of the way of life and expectations of the other. The situation worsened when the bombs failed to fall and there was an increasing feeling that the evacuees were there under false pretences.

By the end of September 1939, many evacuees had returned to Liverpool. A number of factors contributed to this retreat, one of the main ones being the failure of air attack to materialise. For mothers who had gone with children evacuation brought additional pressures. Most prominent among these was the economic difficulty of keeping two homes going cut off as they were from family and community networks and financial supports such as pawnbrokers, local money lenders and access to credit.

Because of the outbreak of war, the re-opening of Liverpool schools had been deferred and they remained closed even after many of the evacuee children had returned to the city. It soon became clear that there were enormous problems associated with the continuation of this situation. Great concern was expressed that children were running wild and unsupervised through the streets of the city. On 16 November 1939, a petition was submitted to the education authorities from 'the parents of Liverpool scholars' pressing for the re-opening of the schools. The same day, a letter was received from the Merseyside Chamber of Commerce, urging the same because of the danger to themselves and others and the annoyance to shopkeepers, of children playing in the streets.[15] As early as 16 September a schoolteacher wrote:

5

'The local Education Committee has been sharply criticised by parents, because of the neglect of children's training... I wish someone would decide to send us back to school because my class and the others are surely as worthy of education as those evacuated.'[16]

With increasing pressure from parents and women's organisations, the Education Committee came to accept that the schools would have to be re-opened, but because of government regulations, adequate ARP had to be provided before this could happen. This would take time, and so pending re-opening, the Education Committee approved the operation of schemes for the supervised home instruction of 27,000 elementary school children.[17]

Evacuation aroused the nation's conscience with its revelations of the conditions of social deprivation that much of the population of the northern industrial areas existed in. For individual women it imposed the burden of deciding whether or not to send their children away alone or endanger their lives by causing them to remain. School closures increased pressures upon them as the care of children left in the city was thrown back totally on the home. All this was happening often at a time when conscription had taken away the father and supervision became, even more than usual, the sole role of the mother.

As well as the difficulties of evacuation, and its associated problems, there were many other new pressures that women had to try to cope with following the declaration of war. In particular, the reverberations of conscription were profound. There was the emotional stress of the physical break-up of the family and the underlying fear for husband or son. Additionally, conscription often brought material hardships. Increased financial difficulties often went hand in hand with the loss of the main breadwinner and/or adult sons. A Mass Observation Report stated: 'Conscription creates a situation where the housewife is left to provide for her children and keep her home going with inadequate support from Army allowance.'[18] For a married woman with two children the 'wife's portion' amounted to 25/- (£1.25) a week,[19] at a time when a man's average weekly earnings in, for example, the drink, food and tobacco processing industries has been estimated at 3.15s (£3.75) a week.[20] Added to this, the increased unemployment among women workers, meant many women no longer had access to income earned on their own account. It is not surprising, therefore, that one of the main problems facing many women in the first few months of war, was the very basic one of making ends meet. Government Orders in Council made provision for a Debt Moratorium to protect the families of serving men. Under this, for example, families were protected from eviction if their allowances were inadequate to meet rental payments. Similar cover prevented the seizure of furniture obtained under hire purchase agreements and made allowances for the suspension of mortgage payments. However, I have found no evidence of implementation of this moratorium and general ignorance even of its existence.[21]

The first year of war made itself forcefully felt in other areas of the everyday lives of Liverpool women. One of the most traumatic elements of those initial months was the blackout—darkness was total and at that time provided the greatest threat to civilian life. Road accidents increased and others were caused by people walking into canals or falling down steps. Shopping was difficult because shops closed earlier to avoid the blackout. From October hand torches were permitted and from then on regulations were gradually relaxed. Apart from the actual dangers of the darkness, there were too the limitations it placed upon the physical mobility of people. A woman typist in Liverpool reported: 'The principle blackout effect is that I am kept indoors a lot ... I used to go to the theatre a lot with my friends but many of them are reluctant to leave their homes.'[22]

Inconvenience multiplied and in the absence of any combat, perhaps created tensions and stresses in addition to their physical effects. War was wearying: difficulties of rationing, rising prices, queues for everything and depleted transport weighed heavily on women's lives, as is illustrated in the general air of depression enclosed in the diary entry of an office worker for 18 December 1940: 'Life at the moment is all bed and work. Going out in the mornings in the moonlight is one of the things I hate ... I am tired of housework, cooking, buying, washing.'[23]
And for January 1941:

> 'No bread, potatoes, meat to be had. Children not going to school. Shortage of coal—people seen taking it from railway stations in prams. Saw a lot of sacks in the tram. People still walking to work on tram routes—hordes marching down London Road.'[24]

There were more subtle changes also, women were seen smoking in the street and trousers were worn by everybody. Gradually, however, as confidence returned, cinemas and theatres began to re-open and something approaching normality re-entered everyday lives as the population gradually adapted to the War, even whilst not accepting easily, the changes it forced upon them.

Perhaps the best summary of the initial impact of the War is included in a Mass Observation Report written in July 1940, which looked retrospectively

7

at the first year of war and found women living lives in which:

'...Compulsion is often disguised as voluntary action, in which women are experiencing the greatest changes in their lives that they could ever imagine; the woman in the home is undergoing much that is difficult and undermining to health and morale; evacuation, conscription, air-raids, the struggle to live, the need to work—all these things are making an indelible effect on her mind, determining her outlook and attitude to everything from rationing to religion, from leisure habits to death.'[25]

FOOTNOTES

1. *Liverpool Gas Company Co-Partners Magazine*, April 1944.
2. Liverpool Council of Social Services, *Bulletin No. 22 : Women and National Service*. 5 September 1939.
3. Trades Union Congress, *Women in the Trade Union Movement*.London, 1955, p.81.
4. Oral evidence 1. Woman, September 1984.
5. Director of Education, *Report on the Evacuation of Liverpool Schools Under the Government Scheme*, presented to Liverpool Education Committee, 25 September 1939.
6. Mass Observation *Extract from Diary*, 3 September 1939.
7. R. Titmuss, *Problems of Social Policy*, HMSO, 1950, p.108.
8. Oral evidence 2. Woman, August 1986.
9. Oral evidence 2.
10. Oral evidence 2.
11. Medical Officer of Health, *Report on Evacuees*, September 1939.
12. Oral evidence 3. Woman, June 1986.
13. Mass Observation, *Extract from Diary*, 1 September 1939.
14. Oral evidence 2. As with so many other aspects of the black experience in Britain, the impact of evacuation on black children, warrents further study.
15. Primary Education Sub-Committee *Minutes*, 25 September 1939.
16. Mass Observation, *Extact from Diary*, 16 September 1939.

17. Primary Education *Minutes*, 25 September 1939.

18. Mass Observation, Report No. 290, *Women in Wartime*, July 1940.

19. Council of Social Service, *Bulletin No. 32 The Wife's Portion*, 21 September 1939.

20. Gertrude Williams, *Women-and Work*, London 1945, p.70.

21. Liverpool Council of Social Services, *Bulletin No. 28, Protection for Families of Serving Men*, 13 September 1939.

22. Mass Observation, *Report No. 290*.

23. Mass Observation, *Extract from Diary*, 18 December 1939.

24. Mass Observation, *Extract from Diary, 29 January 1940*.

25. Mass Observation, *Report No. 290*.

```
COOKING FATS
INCLUDING
LARD AND
DRIPPING
2
```

Women in the Front Line

During 1940, the full horror of total war entered Britain with the commencement of German air attacks. The first Merseyside casualty was on 9 August 1940. Although there had been earlier alarms there had been no systematic large scale attack. However, from August through to November raids were steady, and though many were small and did little or no damage, cumulatively they had a considerable impact on the population. Shelter life became an integral part of everyday living.

In March 1940, because of a steel shortage and the fact that only a quarter of the population had gardens in which they could be put, production of Anderson shelters was abandoned and the Government turned to the production of surface shelters. These were built of brick and concrete and intended to protect the residents of a single street or block of flats. They were, however, very unpopular and widely criticised by those expected to use them. They were put up quickly and shoddily. One of their main problems was that cement shortages were compensated for by substitution with lime rather than by dilution as the Government had suggested. Not surprisingly, some of them fell down: '...I was terrified of the bombs. We used to sit under the table and stairs if we couldn't make it to the big shelter. Them surface ones were no safer than the house.'[1] Other shelter problems were caused by lack of ventilation and the fact that they were generally cold, dark and damp. Mass Observation noted that Liverpool people had 'observably little confidence in the surface shelters available, so they shelter in the often-condemned houses and make the best of it.' As one of the many women who would not use a surface shelter put it ... 'we have no fur coats to keep us warm and after all our stairs are warm even if the house has been condemned these five years'.[2] The same report goes on to say: '... Liverpool shelters are inadequate. In considerable areas there are still practically none. There is little confidence in surface shelters and those built are bitterly cold as they have no doors and the wind whistles straight through them.'[3] Most of the public shelters used as the war proceeded were improvised in basements. Very often the people just needed the security of knowing others were there and sometimes they congregated in places that were no safer than their own homes or were perhaps more dangerous.

Through the autumn months it became customary for those women without their own shelters to make their way in the late afternoon to the public shelters for the night. They were accompanied by their children and often, if the father was still working in Liverpool, he would join them straight from work and go home only the next morning to wash for work again. Disruptive though this type of routine was, the nightly trek to the shelters offered a greater feeling of security for many and might guarantee an undisturbed night's sleep for some, no matter how uncomfortable. Indeed, the conditions in many of the public shelters in those first months of air raids were very bad. A skilled social worker, writing in January 1941, following the worst of the 'Christmas raids', said that in nearly all the large basement shelters:

'... Improvised arrangements, judging by conditions revealed on Merseyside, have created conditions for many citizens which abolish most of the improvements in sanitation, cleanliness and health, made during the last century. The squalor revealed in some of the shelters visited was almost Hogarthian.'[4]

Fear and anxiety became very much part of daily life. Between August and December 1940, 1,081 people were killed and 1,094 seriously injured in Liverpool.[5] One woman told me:

'... My mam was terrified, she used to drive us mad. Even if there was no alert she'd cook the dinner in the afternoon and then carry it out to the shelter, so, when we came home from work we had to go straight down there. I used to pray the sirens would go before I left work so I could stay there with the other girls—I hated that shelter. All the war, my Mam wouldn't let us listen to the radio in case a German plane was passing overhead and homed in on it. She was really frightened.'[6]

Fear of death or injury was only one aspect of air attack. The 'all-clear' might bring relief, for the moment, from the threat of sudden death, but emergence from below ground often meant the beginning of new hardships. Perhaps the loss of friends or relatives who had not been so fortunate or the return to a family home which was now just a pile of bricks and rubble. Being 'bombed out' could mean a lot more than the material loss of house and furniture:

> '...My mother never really got over the house being bombed. I was only a kid then and you don't realise ... I've thought about it since. All she had to show was in that house, she was fanatical about housework and it had taken years to get the furniture and stuff together. I think the piano hurt most—it had come from my Dad's mother's ... no-one could play it but she polished it like it was the crown jewels. (laughing) She was so proud of it, not many where we lived had a piano and there it was smashed and buried. She was never the same after ... Starting again from scratch ...'[7]

Following the initial tremendous emotional shock of the loss of a home and belongings, there was then the immediate and pitiful necessity of finding food, shelter, clothing, warmth and all the many essential things so generally taken for granted. Usually, being bombed out involved a heart rending trek from agency to agency in an attempt to gain assistance. Throughout the war there was no centralised help available for the homeless. Rest Centres provided temporary shelter and meals but were intended to serve only for a few days, this help though was often stretched, by necessity, into weeks. The Government, terrified of these places becoming in any way permanent refuges for families, refused even to provide blankets for them. The Rest Centres were run by an army of dedicated voluntary workers, many of them WVS women, stimulated to help by the all too apparent distress of those in need. E.R. Chamberlain points out that some of these women were technically breaking the law by 'defying government edicts' and supplying those in need with bedding, fuel and food.[8] '... I don't know where those women got their energy from. They never seemed to stop and the same faces seemed to be there all the time.'[9]

For the woman who was 'bombed out' and whose husband was away from home the problems multiplied. Just to obtain the documentation necessary for her to begin to pick up the threads of her life again (ration books, registration papers, etc.) involved a trek to perhaps half-a-dozen government offices in different parts of the city. If she had children she would have to take these with her often when transport services were dislocated by the after effects of air raids. If her family had become separated, the Citizen's Advice Bureau had to be visited, and generally revisited time and time again in an effort to re-establish contact with relatives or to find out what had happended to them. Destruction of household belongings involved initial application to local authorities who might redirect the applicant to the Public Assistance Board. All this on top of the trauma of being bombed out, the uncertainty of the future, the burden of having to cope with confused and distressed children and the stress of having to relate her story several times over in an attempt to get help.

Not all of the official assistance was given without discrimination as is shown in a report for 1941 by the Womens' War Service Bureau. The Bureau had opened a War Distress Clothing Department in Liverpool in November 1940, to provide clothing for families who had lost their possessions in air raids, but it was the intention of the Committee to: '... confine their efforts to making provision for people who have been used to, or can appreciate good clothes'.[10] However, the Committee had found that not many people of 'this type' had wanted them and therefore they had in reserve (this in December 1941 following the havoc of the May Blitz) 'a considerable stock of clothing, suitable for gentle people, to be drawn upon when required'. The Report went on to note that 'generous gifts of clothing' had been received from overseas and—'... Some had been earmarked for bombed families, others for distribution at the Committee's discretion. Clothing varied in quality, part excellent and part suitable for poor families only.'[11] There was also less obvious discrimination: the more literate and articulate of the community were better able to interpret, understand and find their way through all the red tape attached to the whole system of aid for the victims of air attacks. The only help that was fairly easy to obtain, though means tested, was the issue of travel vouchers, by the Public Assistance Committee, to enable the homeless to travel to relatives, thus relieving the local authority of any further responsibility.

Other discrimination was even more explicit. In September 1939, the Government announced the provision of grants 'in respect to physical injury to civilians as a direct result of air raids or other warlike operations'.[12] Injury allowances were not means tested and were to be payable at a weekly rate which was to vary with the size of the family and whether the victim was treated at home or in hospital. Rates were to vary also with the degree of physical disablement but were to be a maximum of 32/6 (£1.62½) a week for a single man and 22/6 (1.12½) a week for a single woman.[13] Compensation for civilian war injuries was increased in December 1940 but continued to be consistently lower for women than for men even in the case of Civil Defence

13

volunteers injured while on duty, often alongside or in identical circumstances to male volunteers. For a man not in hospital compensation was paid at a rate of 35/- (£1.75) a week whilst for a woman, in the same circumstances, it was 28/- (£1.40).[14] These decisions were made at a time when women were driving ambulances, running Rest Centres, arranging the distribution of food and other relief, rescuing people, digging out bodies, tending the injured and generally preventing the collapse of the fabric of society.

In Liverpool, the first of the 'Christmas raids' began in the early evening of 20 December 1940. Fires swept rapidly out of control in the city and many buildings were destroyed. Seeing the fire over the city from her home in Crosby a woman recorded for Mass Observation:

> '...Twelve midnight. Still going strong. Have just been out. Terrific fire over Liverpool. Flames dropping red and green—all colours, just like day...Grand firework display. Search-lights on now. With a fire like that its no use trying to disguise the place. We could actually see the shells bursting in the sky.'[15]

Not everyone, however, thought of the air raids in such picturesque terms, and this woman's observations are obviously influenced by the fact that her area was not, at that time, the target of the attack.

No. 2 *Rescue workers at Old Edge Hill College, Durning Road. Menvale Street in the background. Clint Road front.* Photo by J.E. Marsh, 30th November 1940

The safety of the shelters proved to be an illusion for many that night, as it was repeatedly to be throughout the country during the blitz period. On 28 November 1940, 180 people were killed whilst sheltering under the Junior Technical School in Durning Road. Similarly in December of the same year, an unofficial shelter beneath some railway arches in Bentinck Street, received a direct hit. It was crowded with people and many were buried. Rescue was difficult because the arches had collapsed in huge concrete blocks and it took several days to extricate the 42 bodies of the people killed there. The following night, in an even bigger raid, 74 people were killed when a large shelter received a direct hit.[16] A woman, then 22, and orphaned that week, related:

> '...Mum and Dad were sitting either side of me, there was too much noise to sleep. Winnie and our Kathleen had had an argument so they weren't speaking. I don't remember what happened, my eyes and mouth and all of me were thick with muck and stuff. I couldn't turn over to see if Dad was there but Mum was just gone—you know, not there. I don't know how I got out'.[17]

Another woman recalled:

> '...I remember one night, a raid started before we left work and we were anchored there until it finished even though our shift had finished...Next morning two of the girls were missing. They'd gone home together because they lived in the same street and found a direct hit had taken both their families! There was nothing we could do...what could you say?"[18]

Following the raids over the Christmas period, the attacks slackened but in March and April they increased in severity and incidence. Even during 'quiet' periods, the ever-present fear that 'they' might come over that night meant anxiety diminished little. Death seemed so indiscriminate most felt at risk:

> '...I lost my little girl at that time. I've always believed it was the bombing...She was such a pretty child. We'd be huddled under the stairs and she used to be in total terror. She'd screw up her eyes and push her fists into her ears and sometimes get her head under my skirt...there was no comforting her...No-one will ever convince me she didn't die of fright and the fear of it all.'[19]

Sometimes the sirens sounded, those who had risked staying at home that night rushed to the shelters and the all-clear might later sound without there having been any actual attack. Broken nights and lack of sleep were major sources of stress. Nevertheless, despite this, Mass Observation found, '...Morale in Liverpool appreciably higher than in other blitzed towns' although: ' ... In all classes there is widespread rather despairing contempt for the City Council and its alleged corruptions which has increased lately since the City was now governed by an Emergency Committee of three, with the shipowner—mayor in the chair'.[20]

1 May 1941 saw the onset of eight successive nights of raids in what became known as the May Blitz. During eight days and nights, 1,453 people were killed in Liverpool alone and more than 1,000 seriously injured. In Liverpool and the surrounding districts, 90,000 homes were destroyed, about 40 per cent. of the total housing stock. The heart was torn from the city and the dockland areas were devastated. The civic authorities had to deal with 51,000 homeless people and the problem was further aggravated by many of the Rest Centres being put out of action.[21] People began to evacuate themselves each afternoon to the outlying areas of the City, creating massive problems of control which greatly troubled the local authority. By 9 May 1941, emergency measures had resulted in 10,000 homeless people being billeted in reception centres outside the city boundries but this still left a great many people unprovided for. The numbers of the official homeless were further swelled by those rendered temporarily homeless by the danger of unexploded bombs, but who had no claim on official assistance because, technically, they still had their homes.

Nightly evacuation or 'trekking' continued to be a problem. On 15 May 1941, the Civil Defence Emergency Committee received a report that approximately 4,500 people were still travelling nightly from Liverpool to Huyton and were greatly taxing the area's resources. The Committee agreed to do all it could to discourage people from leaving the area and if they continued to do so to 'transport them back'.[22] On 16 May 1941 it was resolved that from 19 May, nightly evacuees were not to be admitted to Rest Centres in Maghull, Huyton and Prescot unless carrying a certificate of homelessness.[23] A Mass Observation Report of 22 May found:

> '... Universal criticism and dissatisfaction with post blitz administration stronger in Liverpool than any other town ... A situation of doubt and rumour—almost complete absence of information and explanation ... A loudspeaker van toured but only to give information about transport services'.[24]

Outside the city boundaries, rumours of martial law in Liverpool were common and although having no basis in fact, their existence illustrates the lack of communication about what was actually happening.

The last raid on Merseyside was 10 January 1942. Throughout, women had been in the forefront of those attacked and of those who worked unceasingly to aid the bereaved and homeless. In the Summer of 1940, the Women's Voluntary Service had sponsored its Housewives' Service which was intended to train women, whose family ties prevented them taking part in regular Civil Defence, in simple first aid and air raid precautions so that they could offer assistance to neighbours during and following air raids. In October 1940, the Daily Post reported that more than a thousand women had attended lectures and were due to be issued with membership cards.[25]

No. 3 WVS worker serving refreshments to rescue workers, St. Georges Crescent and Lord Street, May 1941. Photo: J.E. Marsh

The women of the WVS dealt compassionately and efficiently with a multitude of frequently-tragic problems from doing washing for those who had been bombed out to sorting personal belongings and scraps of material which might help to identify people killed in raids. On 1 May 1949, twelve WVS workers engaged in preparing meals for the homeless were killed; it will never be known exactly how many other women gave their lives in quiet acts of service. The Blitz showed, beyond a doubt, the courage and efficiency of

17

women Civil Defence workers, at a time when the State was paying them compensation for injuries received on duty at a rate of two-thirds that paid to men. This did not pass unnoticed: indeed, the only organised lobby against the Bill for the conscription of women came from women who demanded that: '...in the event of conscription becoming law, the Government should undertake to give men and women equal pay for equal work and equal compensation for injuries received as the result of enemy action.'[26]

Throughout the period of aerial attack, many many women came out from their shelters, salvaged what they could from heaps of rubble that were once their homes, identified their dead, attended the mass funerals, comforted their friends and relatives and all this against a background of constant uncertainty and anxiety. Not knowing what was happening to husbands, sons and friends abroad fighting or as prisoners and often in the more despairing knowledge that they were 'missing' or killed in action; these women carried on with the daily routines of shopping, working and caring for their families.

FOOTNOTES

1. **Oral evidence 4. Woman, September 1980.**

2. **Mass Observation,** *Report No. 538, Liverpool and Manchester Blitz,* January 1941.

3. Mass Observation, *Report No. 538.*

4. Mass Observation, *Report No. 538.*

5. Daily Post and Echo Ltd., *Bombers Over Merseyside–The Authorative Record of the Blitz,* 1943.

6. Oral evidence 5. Woman, August 1980.

7. Oral evidence 6. Woman, November 1983.

8. E.R. Chamberlain, *Life in Wartime Britain,* London 1972, p.68.

9. Oral evidence 7. Man, June 1983.

10. *Annual Report of the Women's War Service Bureau,* 1 January - 31 December 1941.

11. *Report Women's War Service Bureau.*

12. Liverpool Council of Social Service, *Bulletins No. 31, Victims of Air Raids,* 20 September 1939.

13. Liverpool Council of Social Service, *Bulletin No. 31*.

14. Liverpool Council of Social Service, *Bulletin No. 31*.

15. Mass Observation, *Extract from Diary*, 27 December 1941.

16. Liverpool Daily Post & Echo Ltd. *Bombers Over*.

17. Oral evidence 8. Women, January 1981.

18. Oral evidence 9. Women, October 1980.

19. Oral evidence 10. Woman,

20. Mass Observation, *Report No. 538*.

21. Liverpool Daily Post and Echo Ltd., *Bombers Over*.

22. Civil Defence Emergency Committee *Minutes* 15 May 1941.

23. Civil Defence Emergency Committee *Minutes* 16 May 1941.

24. Mass Observation, *Report No. 706*, May 1941.

25. Daily Post, 21 October 1940.

26. Dr. E. Summerskill, 'Conscription and Women', *The Fortnightly*, March 1942.

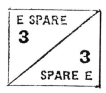

Women at work

As we have seen, the potential value of women's labour was not quickly recognised. On 10 May 1940, following a period of increasing crisis, the Chamberlain Government resigned and a new era in the course of the war began under the government leadership of Churchill. The new Government requested, and was granted, greater powers than were implicit in the emergency legislation of the beginning of the war. The worth of British women gradually became apparent and, in January 1941, they were called upon to take an even more active part in the war effort.

From the second half of 1940, the services had begun to step up demands for recruits and it rapidly became clear that these demands could only be met by the withdrawal of men from industry. In turn, massive numbers of new troops necessitated the expansion of arms production to equip them—the Government turned to women. Government Training Centres were set up and, to cope in the meantime, a policy of dilution was agreed with the Trade Unions. In January 1941, the Minister of Labour and National Service, Ernest Bevin, announced '...We have now reached the stage where...we shall call into service many women, who in normal circumstances, would not take employment.'[1] In March 1941, the compulsory registration of women aged twenty to twenty-one years was begun and by the end of the year had been extended to include women up to 30 years of age. But powers over women were used only with reluctance and appeals for volunteers continued to be paramount well into 1941. In February 1941, the Evening Express reported

20

that Miss C. Haslett, Advisor to the Minister of Labour, had appealed to Merseyside women to render greater effort in the nation's war effort, because there was an immediate need for 7,000 women to undertake war work in local factories. The same news report included an exhortation from the Chairman of the Merseyside Labour Supply Committee: 'The sooner you enter industry and turn out the materials required, the sooner the War will be over, with our menfolk at home and evacuated children at their own firesides. We want all classes of women.'[2] Yet despite appeals, voluntary enrolment did not produce the desired effect.

No. 4 *Appeal for women to volunteer for work in the munitions industry.*

Recruitment for the munitions industries was, at least partially, particularly difficult; 'many women preferred to work in the civilian industries where hours of work were shorter and wages sometimes higher'.[3] They were also unpopular because of the transport difficulties associated with working in locations, so far outside the cities. In their early stages there was a shortage of welfare facilities and women were fearful of explosions, dermatitis and skin discolouration. Whatever the reasons, workers were very difficult to get and wastage rates were high. When first planned, it had been expected that workers would leave their homes and live in hostels near the factory site, but it quickly became apparent that many of the operatives couldn't and wouldn't leave their homes as they had family responsibilities.[4]

On 18 December 1941, the National Service (No.2) Act became law; the unprecedented step of conscription of women, for military and industrial service had begun. Single women between twenty and twenty-one years of age were made liable for military service. Nineteen year olds were brought in the following year. All the women conscripted would be able to choose between the:

> '... auxiliary services or important jobs in industry. Those who opted for the former would not be posted to combatant duties unless they volunteered for them. With this formula, the Act gained general acceptance. The Wartime Social Survey found 97 per cent. of women agreed emphatically that women should undertake war work.'[5]

Women with children under fourteen years were exempted from the law and every woman had the right to claim exemption if she could show her call-up would interfere with her husband's war work. Even those women exempted, though, were strongly urged to enter some sort of war work.

For years, employers had strongly and consistently resisted calls to introduce part-time working so one of the more ironic elements of conscription was its introduction. Before the war many married women had unsuccessfully sought the opportunity of doing paid work which would fit in with household duties. During the war part-time working was insisted upon. In December 1941, Churchill said:

> '... The part-time employment of women in industry has already been developed but nothing like on the scale which must be reached in the months which lie before us ... an immense variety of arrangements are possible to enable women to divide up domestic tasks and then be free to work, close at hand, in the factory or field. The treatment of the problem must be flexible.'[6]

The conscription of women necessarily involved an acceptance of the particular problems faced by women who undertook the dual role of unpaid domestic labour and paid industrial work, which imposed a double burden on

REGISTRATION FOR EMPLOYMENT ORDER, 1941

MINISTRY OF LABOUR AND NATIONAL SERVICE

Local Office..
CONGREG.....AL SCHOOLS,
PORTL......STREET,
5|12|41   SOUTH....(Date)T

National Registration Identity No. | NHxB | 2qq | 3 |

NATIONAL WORK NOTICE

Dear Madam,

As a result of your registration under the Registration for Employment Order, 1941, you are considered to be available for vital war work of the type set out in form E.D.L. 74 which you have received. Your name has accordingly been entered on the National Work Register.

You will be expected to take up such work or service of national importance in whichever district it is available, and arrangements will now be made to assist you to do so. If, in the meantime, you change your address you should inform this Office.

This notice is issued by order of the Minister of Labour and National Service under Article 2 (*b*) of the Registration for Employment Order, 1941.

Yours faithfully,

T.PH.

Manager.

Miss .... Lily Harrison ....

.... 3 Selworthy Rd, ...

.... Birkdale ....

E.D. 381.   Southport.

(14597) Wt. 25959—9626 500m 9/41 D.L. G. 373

No. 5 Lily Harrison was conscripted from her position as domestic servant in a Southport household to work in Kirkby Munitions Factory.

many. A change in social attitudes towards the employment of married women was essential. In the period before the war, a woman who married and decided to continue in work was often subject to extreme social pressures and she had to go deliberately against accepted practice. Husbands were generally very reluctant to allow their wives to continue in full-time paid employment outside the home because of the implicit stigma they felt it carried in relation to their own ability to provide for their wives. In any case, Liverpool employers didn't generally allow women to continue working after marriage! '... You had to leave as soon as you got married, although I managed to stay until I got pregnant. I hung my wedding ring round my neck and didn't crack on'[7] However, others didn't find it quite so easy to conceal their new status:

> '... My chap and me were working together and we weren't going to say... I stayed off on the Monday to help clear up after the wedding, but I intended going in the next day; however, someone snitched and they called my chap into the office and said 'Tell your wife to send in her tally and collect her cards'. So that was that.'[8]

During the war, government propaganda completely reversed the situation and women who did not assume some sort of work on top of their household duties felt guilty, apologetic and anxious to justify themselves.

The growth of mass production and light engineering in the Inter-War years had increasingly meant the employment of women for repetitive work; usually single women before marriage. Employers took advantage of their ability to do fine, monotonous work very cheaply and therefore, unlike in 1914, there were many thousands of women already experienced in factory work and not all these women were anxious to return to it. It is important to remember that freedom to work outside the home was a form of emancipation that many working class women would readily forego. As Gertrude Williams recognised:

> '... Practically all working class girls are compelled to earn their living in the interval between school and marriage; for them paid work has not been a symbol of emancipation but a stern and often regretted necessity. The woman wage-earner has not looked upon her industrial occupation as a career, nor as an opportunity to express her individuality, nor as the means of providing herself with an honourable alternative to marriage. Neither the types of work in which women have been employed, nor the wages and conditions afforded them, have been such as to cast any glamour

over earning a living. When marriage, home and children offered themselves as an alternative, industrial work could be sacrificed without a pang.'[9]

And as Mass Observation recorded: 'Few working-class women who go into industry through necessity, do so except to supplement their housekeeping and allowance.'[10] The Government, therefore, had to change public attitudes to married women workers and to convince the women themselves that their duty lay not in the home (as previously presumed) but at the work bench. The stimulation of patriotic fervour, while important, was not enough, as was illustrated by the lack of response to appeals for voluntary labour in the period before conscription. The State was forced into an acceptance that the roots of economic and social disadvantage from which women suffered might be found in the dual role they play in society and so had to attempt some amelioration of this situation.

Perhaps the most demanding aspects of married women's lives are the duties associated with the care of young children. State recognition of this fact was implicit in the massive wartime increase in the provision of nursery facilities. Initially wartime nurseries were an offshoot of the evacuation programme—to relieve pressure on households where young children were billeted, but their main stimulus came in industrial areas where the aim was to free mothers for war work. In Liverpool, in 1939, there was accommodation for 161 children in voluntary nurseries but, at the outbreak of war, these closed and although the Adam Cliff and Everton Road Nurseries re-opened in 1940, six nursery classes in primary schools remained closed.[11] However, when in July 1941 the National Government started its campaign to recruit women on a massive scale to produce war materials and to release men and women without ties for work in the services, the provision of nurseries became crucial.

On 18 November 1941, the Liverpool Daily Post announced Liverpool's plans for wartime nurseries. The authorities were to provide two types of child care. For children of two to five years there were to be part-time nursery classes, which were open the same times as schools, and full-time day nurseries which were for children of all ages up to five years. These latter were to be open 8.00 a.m. to 5.00 p.m., and on Saturday mornings. It was estimated that accommodation would be available for 500 children.[12]

As recruitment was stepped up and conscription introduced, there was increasing demand for nursery accommodation and the local authority was hard pressed to keep up. There were great problems attached to equipping nurseries at a time when there were severe restrictions on the use of materials. Staffing, also, was a major problem. Training schemes were set up but industry offered better wages and terms. On 9 October 1941, it was reported that it had proved impossible to engage Probationers for the Everton Road Nursery; at the rate of pay offered, 10/- (50p) a week and so it had been necessary to offer 15/- (75p) a week, plus bonus (dinners and teas)![13] Nevertheless, the opening of child care centres, for the under fives, went ahead and in Liverpool by 1944 there was accommodation for 2,445 children.

Even at its peak, the nursery provision in Liverpool did not meet demand. There were always waiting lists at most of the nurseries and in July 1944 the Liverpool Daily Post reported that 700 children in Liverpool were still awaiting places.[14] Apart from the actual difficulty of obtaining places, women war workers had other problems associated with placing their children in nurseries. In March 1942 Mass Observation completed a report on the 'Demand for Day Nurseries' and found that very often they were situated too far from home and work and the hours were too short to be of any real help. They also did nothing to solve the problem of what to do with younger children of school age whose school hours did not fit in with factory shifts, the report concluded, though, that day nurseries were on the whole welcomed by mothers.[15]

Welcomed they may have been, but nursery schools did not relieve mothers of their responsibilities to anything like the degree commonly supposed. A lot of time was taken up in taking children to and from the nursery, and there were still many tasks to be done in which the schools gave no assistance. In the days before washing machines were commonplace in ordinary homes and easy-care fabrics were unheard of, a major proportion of a mother's time was spent in washing and ironing—in winter drying clothes was very difficult. Even where the money was available, rationing meant that clothes were not easily replaced when torn so had to be repaired, socks had to be darned, trousers and dresses patched and woollies knitted. If a child was ill he or she couldn't attend nursery and so the mother had to stay home also. So it may be seen that, although child care facilities were a great improvement on what was available pre-war, they were very basic and left a lot of mother's problems untouched.

Despite their disadvantages, it would seem that the report in one newspaper of the comments of a mother of a two year old is typical of the general attitude towards wartime nurseries: '... It's the best thing that has ever happened. I could not buy the little luxuries I wanted to for Ann out of an Army Allowance. Why! Before I started work I had to count the coppers 'ere buying a bag of apples; now everything runs smoothly.'[16]

As noted earlier, though, not all who wanted them obtained nursery places. Most of the children of war workers seem to have been looked after by relatives or neighbours and some by Registered Child Minders. The latter, however, was never a very important area of child care provision during the war period. In April 1943, it was reported that in Liverpool, the number of foster-mothers willing to undertake care of children had decreased steadily since the outbreak of war. At the end of 1938, 101 were registered while by 1943, there were only 45 and a number of those were refusing to accept further children. It was proposed that advertisements be placed to attract more because of the number of mothers applying for foster-care.[17]

The preparation of meals was yet another duty which took up a great deal of women's time, but the war revolutionised eating habits. Before the war, it was very rare for solid meals to be eaten ouside the home during the day. Very few canteens were available and those there were, were little- used because workers were unaccustomed to eating outside their homes. School meals were only for the necessitous.

> '... The very, very poor—we could have applied for it at that time,
> but people felt the stigma used to get a coupon from school ... for
> that ticket they got a bowl of hot soup and a slice of bread ... and
> you had to be a pauper to get it and of course you run the gauntlet
> going up there with all kids making fun at you.'[18]

Invariably, women had to spend a good proportion of their time shopping for, preparing and cooking main meals. However, wartime regulations led to the provision of supervised canteens in factories and workers were encouraged to eat a hot meal at midday. The number of children eligible for school meals was vastly extended and British or Civic Restaurants 'constituted a new phenomenon in communal life'.[19] They grew out of the communal feeding centres provided for the victims of air raids but were soon set up on a wider and more permanent basis, providing good, plentiful meals at low cost. The habit developed of 'eating out' and so for many women, the time spent cooking was proportionately reduced.

No. 6 *British restaurant under the railway arches, Athol Street.*

Once the value of women's labour had been recognised, Mr. Bevin, the Minister of Labour, began his drive to restructure the workforce. To this end he employed Caroline Haslett as his Honorary Adviser and appointed an advisory committee comprised of labour women, women M.P's and other women leaders to 'advise the Minister of Labour and National Service on questions affecting the recruitment and registration of women and on the best methods of securing their service for the war effort.'[20] This body later became responsible for policies relating to every aspect of women's work in the war industries. Women entered almost every sector of employment with the exception of coal mining and dock labour.

Not all women changed their jobs, some jobs were modified to fit in with wartime requirements, as one woman who worked in Barker and Dobson's (the sweet manufacturers) recalled:

> ... We were doing the same job only now I was packing sweets for
> the NAAFI. We had a good time there. They had great big tins of

fruit and we often got away with some—everbody did. I loved it there.'[21]

Many private companies changed over to war production. In Liverpool the football pool and mail order firm of Littlewoods went over to the production of barrage balloons. The women there worked twelve hour shifts, four days 'on', two days 'off', followed by four nights 'on'. It may be seen then that factory work could have been very demanding both physically and mentally, especially for those not used to it. Working hours were expected to be longer during the war as shown by a War Bulletin of April 1940:

'There is bound to be a relaxation of the new Factories Act, where women were limited to 48 hours a week to which six hours overtime may be added, because EFFECTIVE working hours are always less than actual working hours. Grouping all varied munition work together it is suggested that -
1.   For those in which there is much handwork, a 48 hour week or less is probably the optimum.
2.   Where the element of handwork is small, there should be a 54 hour week.
3.   A 51-54 hour week should be tried.

Hours are greater than those which are best for peacetime, but in wartime there will be a certain margin of extra effort because of the incentive of patriotism.'[22]

However, as the war proceeded it became clear that increased working hours were not as productive as initially visualised and another Bulletin of May 1941 states:

'...It has been noted that many more women and girls are now within industry. During recent months many of these workers have been subjected to unaccustomed strains both at home and at their work. The normal holiday and weekend arrangements have of necessity been interrupted and as a result there is a danger of a reduction in productive capacity due to persistent fatigue leading in some cases to a breakdown in health. It is increasingly clear that a break is necessary to prevent illness and incapacity and the Liverpool Union of Girls Clubs has opened a Guest House at Abergele. Because of reluctance to say they are in need of a break the scheme relies on employers, work's doctors, welfare officers and workmates.'[23]

And further:

> '... A report issued by the Industrial Health Research Board on hours of work, lost time and labour wastage, reveals that increased hours of work result in a loss of production per hour. Weekly hours of work shouldn't exceed 60-65 for men and 50-60 for women, as to do so will result in loss of rate of production and often increased absence.'[24]

Actual hours of work were often extended by the amount of time taken to travel to and from work. In an investigation into working conditions in a wartime filling factory, it was found that one and a half hours travelling each was 'normal' and most working days comprised only of travelling, working, eating and sleeping.[25] In winter, the situation was worsened by women having to leave home and return in the dark.

For some women, the war brought welcome changes. A woman who had been in service since she was fourteen years old found work in a local munitions factory:

> 'In a way I was glad of the War, I got a job at nearly three pound a week more . . . I was on filling shells and detonators and you really had to concentrate. I was terrified most of the time—I didn't smoke but lots did and I always had this fear that they wouldn't be able to wait an hour. There were signs up all over the place saying 'No Smoking'. One day there was an explosion and this terrible, terrible screaming. I didn't want to see so I just ran away out of the room. I heard later that she'd had her finger blown off; I suppose that was lucky when you think what an explosion could have done. The screams were terrible.'[26]

Women continued to enter most of the previously exclusive male areas of occupation and the nation continued to pay them at rates much lower than their male counterparts. Throughout the War this fact aroused feminist sentiment everywhere and the injustice of it even permeated the more traditionally formal and respected areas of society. At the end of 1941, the *Financial News* in a leading article pointed out that: ' . . . in every industry, the average earnings of women in July 1941, were less than half those of the men and that the ratio of the increase in women's earnings since 1938 was, in most cases, lower still.'[27]

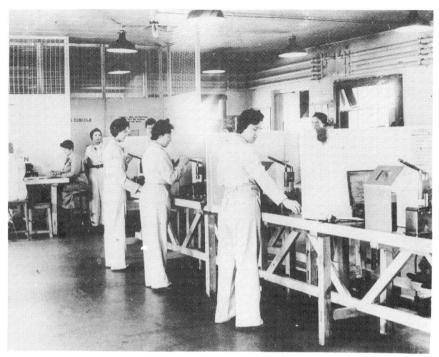

No. 7 *Kirkby munitions workers.*

Equal pay for women was not, however, just a question of social justice. Purely in terms of supply and demand women during the war should have received the same wages as men. In peacetime the occupational openings for women were very limited. The traditional women's jobs such as nursing and domestic service were always poorly paid. The chief work of women in the home was not paid at all and because of the restricted openings available to women in other occupations, the supply of women workers generally exceeded demand so they could be induced to work at lower rates than men. During the war, though, the position of women in the labour market was radically changed, demand for women workers seemed to be out-stripping supply but employers continued to pay women at rates below those of men. In 1940, the average weekly earnings of men in electrical engineering was estimated at 5.5s (£5.25) while for women they were 2.5s (£2.25).[28]

The State was no better an employer in this respect than were employers in the private sector. In October 1941, the National Union of Women Teachers submitted a resolution to the Liverpool Board of Education to protest about the war bonus recommendations of the Burnham Committee:

'. . . which embody the gross injustice of a lower rate of bonus for women teachers than for men..Proposals take no cognisance of the fact that the rise in the cost of living affects all teachers and that, while purporting to make better provisions for lower paid teachers, the new scheme illogically allots lower rates of bonus to women who already receive lower rates of pay than their male colleagues.'[29]

The resolution went on to reiterate its demands for an immediate flat rate bonus of 10/- (50p) weekly for all teachers irrespective of age, scale or sex. At that time rates were between 1/- (5p) and 2s.6d. (12^1_{02}) less for women than for men.[30] Because of the outcry, the question of war bonus for teachers was referred to arbitration but ultimately Burnham Committee recommendations were carried.

Many more women joined trade unions. In 1939 only 15.6 per cent. of women were trade union members but by 1941, this figure had increased to 19.4 per cent.[31] In June 1940, a proposal to admit women to the Amalgamated Engineering Union was defeated but this decision was reversed in January 1943 and women became eligible for membership. By the close of 1943, the AEU had 130,000 women members.[32] On the whole, the unions were anxious to secure men's rates for as many women as possible although generally conditional on women not being taken on while men were available and that after the war men were to be re-instated. Important agreements on the question of equal pay were made. In the Boot and Shoe trade, women replaced men in an industry in which ' . . . exclusively male labour was employed' and were to receive ' . . . the wage rates appropriate to men doing similar work'.[33] In the engineering trades and in transport, substitution at equal pay was also agreed upon. Trade union moves towards obtaining equal pay for women were not, though, without an element of self interest. Many trade unionists appreciated it would be 'safer' for them if women weren't introduced as cheap labour, so they endeavoured to ensure women got the 'rate for the job'. Although providing very important precedents, agreements in theory were very different from what generally actually happened. When the railway companies were challenged by the unions to pay women clerks the 'rate for the job', they replied that '... since the managers had been unable to find any industry where the principle of equal pay for equal work was applied (they) didn't see why they should apply it on the railways.'[34]

Wording often left loopholes which employers were quick to seize upon. In the Royal Ordinance factories, although the categories of women paid under the 'women's schedule' (that is at lower pay than men) were progressively reduced during the war as a result of trade union agitation, in September 1943 nearly three quarters of women employed still came under the women's schedule.[35] This was at a time when women's employment in filling factories was at its peak. Until 1942, 'leads', or ability pay, in the filling factories were standardised at 2/-; 4/-; 6/-; and 8/- for women compared with 2/-; 5/-; 7/6; and 10/- for men.[36] In February 1942, during a debate in the House of Commons, Eleanor Rathbone, a Liverpool MP stated:

> '... While women are supposed to be enjoying the rate for the job, we often find that when a job is offered to a woman, changes are made in the processes to enable the employers to say it is not the same job that a man was doing before, but a different one. Then changes are made in the rate of pay.'[37]

The advance of mass production increasingly broke down skilled work and made it easier for employers to say that there was no pre-war precedent for the type of work the women were doing. Where this didn't happen they could make small alterations to the job and reach the same conclusion. Although there were women who earned male rates under the dilution scheme, in January 1944, '... women in metal work and engineering earned an average of £3.10s. (£3.50) a week to a man's £7.0s.[38]

During the War the question of equal pay for women became a focal point of women's agitation and the whole period was characterised by a fight for economic equality. As seen, many collective agreements had included the principle of equal pay for equal work as an essential condition of the employment of women. Even though agreement had not necessarily resulted in economic equality in many occupations, women had high hopes of achieving implementation at the end of the war. They seemed to have a great deal in their favour. Members of Parliament, the trade unions, economists and public opinion generally had given support to the principle. In 1944 the TUC submitted evidence to the Royal Commission on Equal Pay which had been

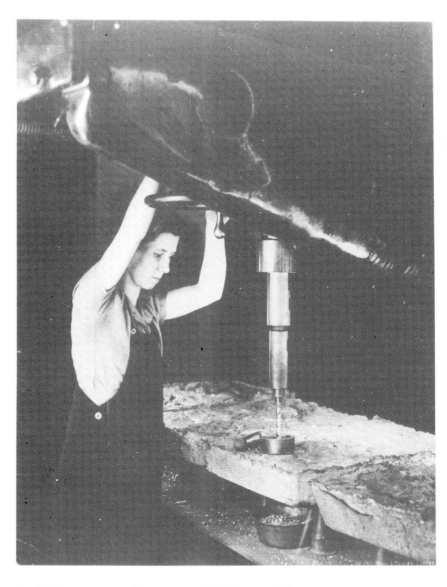

No. 8 *Woman sampling blister copper. BICC Prescot 1943*

formed '... to examine the existing relationship between the renumeration of men and women in the public services, in industry and other fields of employment, to consider the social, economic and financial implications of claims of equal pay for equal work.'[39] Most of the professions had adopted the equal pay principle, in medicine, the law and the press, women were accorded economic equality with men. Following a request from the Minister of Education in March 1944, for evidence that local authorities desired equal terms for men and women teachers, Liverpool City Council informed the Government, '... that such a reform is justified and would be welcomed.'[40] However, the Royal Commission Report on Equal Pay, issued in October 1946, recommended the rejection of the claim for equal pay and dashed hopes that the experience of war had done something to materially alter official attitudes towards the economic position of women within society. Unequal rates of pay for comparable work between men and women remained the general rule.

As indicated above, women were required to leave their jobs in local industry upon marriage. However, industry was not the only sector of the local economy which didn't allow married women to work. The Sex Disqualification Removal Act of 1918 had given some women the vote but had not improved their position in business and the professions. Women employed by the government or local authorities continued to be dismissed upon marriage. The Act meant only that '... an authority was now at liberty to employ married women, but was equally free not to do so.'[41] At the beginning of the War the 'marriage bar' was still an integral part of women's social position, as is illustrated by a case recorded in Liverpool Council Minutes for October 1940. The Public Assistance Officer reported that he had received a request from a female clerk that she be allowed to retain her employment after marriage 'for such time as her services are needed'. Her fiance was an Able Seaman in the Royal Navy and she said she wouldn't marry if it meant losing her job. It was reported that she was paid 35/- (£1.75) a week and her home circumstances weren't good. Her father was in ill-health and working only intermittently and the income of the household was almost wholly comprised of the income of the three daughters. The Committee resolved that the woman's services be retained in view of the circumstances and noted that the Co-ordination (Special) Committee in June 1940 resolved:

'That for the period of the war, employing committees be permitted to employ married women on a temporary basis, where

35

this is necessitated by a shortage of properly qualified labour, or where, in the case of an employee already in the service, the Committee considers the employee's financial circumstances justify this course; provided that all cases shall be reviewed by the employing committees at intervals of not more than six months.'[42]

The many women who during the War continued to be employed by the local authority, were not actually regarded as still being 'in the service': 'A woman teacher who marries ceases to be in the service, but for the duration of the war, may be engaged on a six monthly basis where they have the necessary qualifications and experience . . .'[43] Margaret Goldsmith wrote of cases where permanent civil servants had married: ' . . . and after a short honeymoon had returned to their posts. They were not dismissed because they were married as would have happened earlier. Instead they were 're-instated for the duration'—at a lower salary and in a lower grade.'[44] Their marriages had made them temporary civil servants. However, despite this type of abuse of married women's labour, a precedent had been set. Married women proved themselves to be as capable, responsible and dependable after marriage as before. In 1946, official recognition of this fact was given in the lifting of the 'marriage bar' from women employed in National Government service.

As may be seen, the demands of war brought radical changes into the lives of women workers. Many of the alterations in official attitudes were, however, reversed once the war ended and nowhere can this be seen more clearly than in the provision of child care facilities. In 1943 a Government White Paper, which foreshadowed the 1944 Education Act, included a section on the education of children under compulsory school age. This Paper said that nurseries provided a service which was necessary whether parents worked or not, were of great benefit to the children and influenced parents through the training of their children and through the medical services provided. The Paper anticipated that nurseries would continue and that new ones would be built nearer the children's homes.[45] At the beginning of 1945, the future of nurseries seemed assured but by December 1945, a change of emphasis may be increasingly seen in government literature and the media and the Ministry of Education had announced that changes were to be made in provision for the under fives·

'The Ministry felt that children under two should have their mother's at home with them and should be discouraged from working outside their homes. Day nurseries and daily guardians were to be regarded as provision for special cases only—when mothers had to work, when home conditions were unsuitable or where the mother was incapable for 'some good reason' of looking after her children.'[46]

Despite Liverpool Education Committee protests that there should not be any actual reduction of accommodation until 'existing demands had been met'[47], there was a steady contraction in nursery services from 1945 on. By 1947 there were only thirteen nurseries still in operation in Liverpool with accommodation for 756 children.[48]

Nevertheless, the entry of women into industry on a massive scale did bring about some permanent, if sometimes less measurable changes. Many new professions were opened up associated with factory welfare work and factory inspection in which women played major roles. The State and private employers had been forced to recognise the double burden of paid work outside the home coupled with unpaid domestic work inside the home and to adapt accordingly by allowing time for shopping and by the unprecedented massive increase in part-time employment. Trade union membership by women increased greatly and though after the War, when many women left industry, women's membership fell back, some elements of this remained. The traditional 'craft minded' unions of the Amalgamated Engineering Union and the Electricians Trade Union had admitted women for the first time and once initiated this could not be revoked.

It is not easy to see much emancipation in the entry of most women into full-time paid labour. The work was generally repetitive and tedious and women worked long hours, very often for lower pay than their male colleagues. But some of the changes which endured were positive:

'I'd never had any proper money off him; he was never much good to us even before he went off—I had money of my own for the first time and by God it felt good. I did all sorts with it, new lino . . . when he did come round he had something to say, the eyebrows'd go up, 'You're doing O.K. for yourself.' 'Aye', I thought, 'And no thanks to you.'[49]

As Gertrude Williams argued:

'War has shown how many women welcomed employment as a relief from the monotony and isolation of domestic work. The gossip of the shop, the companionship of fellow workers, the opportunity to see new faces and make new friends are all sources of pleasure.[50]

At the beginning of 1942, Caroline Haslett, when asked what the effects of conscription would be for women after the War had ended, replied that she believed that women had acquired greater confidence in themselves and their ability and would therefore be more articulate in their demands.[51] It is impossible to generalise, clearly the impact of the war years was felt and interpreted differently by individual women according to their experiences. However, perhaps Caroline Haslett's hopes were realised in the increasingly vocal and confident (if largely ignored until the 1970's) efforts of women in the post-war years to obtain economic and social equality.

FOOTNOTES

1. **Trades Union Congress,** *Women in the Trade Union* p.81.
2. *Evening Express,* '7,000 War Workers Wanted', 6 February 1941.
3. P. Inman, *Labour in the Munitions Industry*, HMSO, 1950, p.179.
4. V. Croot Stone, *A study of some social and industrial problems involved in modern, large-scale employment of labour in unskilled work, based on observation and investigation in a wartime filling factory.* M.A. 1945, Liverpool.
5. A Calder, *The People's War–Britain 1939 - 1945*, London, 1971. pp.268-269.
6. W. Churchill, December 1941, quoted in M. Goldsmith, *Women at War*, London, 1943. p.197.
7. Oral evidence 11. Woman, September 1985.
8. Oral evidence 12. Woman, March 1987.
9. Gertrude Williams, *Women at Work*, London 1945, p.49.
10. Mass Observation, *Report No. 290.*
11. Public Health Department, *Report on the Health of the City of Liverpool*, 1939.
12. *Liverpool Daily Post*, 'Wartime Nurseries', 18 November 1941.

13. Liverpool Education Committee *Minutes*, 9 October 1941.

14. *Liverpool Daily Post*, '700 Children waiting for Accommodation', 18 July 1944.

15. Mass Observation, *Report No. 1151, The Demand for Day Nurseries*, 11 March 1942.

16. *Walton Times*, 'Christine Reporting on War Nurseries', 21 October 1943.

17. Maternity and Child Welfare Sub-Committee *Minutes*, 16 April 1943.

18. Oral evidence 13. Man, July 198.

19. Gertrude Williams, *Women at Work*, p.83.

20. Trade Union Congress, *Women in the Trade Union*, p.84.

21. Oral Evidence 10.

22. Council of Social Services, *Bulletin No.42, Hours of Work in Wartime*, April 1940.

23. Council of Social Services, *Bulletin No.51, Rest Breaks for Women Workers*, 17 May 1941.

24. Council of Social Services, *Bulletin No.61, Hours of Work*, 18 May 1942.

25. V. Croot Stone, *A Study*, p.17.

26. Oral evidence 14. Woman, January 1987.

27. Financial News 1941 in Trades Union Congress, *Women in the Trade Union*, p.86.

28. Gertrude Williams, *Women at Work*, pp.70-71.

29. Liverpool Education Committee *Minutes*, 9 October 1941.

30. Liverpool Education Committee *Minutes*, 9 October 1941.

31. Trades Union Congress, *Women in the Trade Union*, p.84.

32. M.A. Hamilton, *Women at Work*, London 1941.

33. A. Calder, *The People's War*, p.402.

34. A. Calder, *The People's War*, p.402.

35. P. Inman, *Labour in the Munitions*, p.354.

36. P. Inman, *Labour in the Munitions*, p.354.

37. E. Rathbone, from a House of Commons debate on the *Restoration of Pre-war Trade Practices Bill*, February 1942.

38. A. Calder, *The People's War*, p.403.

39. Director of Education, *Report on the Subject of Equal Pay for Men and Women Teachers*, May 1944.

40. Director of Education, *Report on Equal Pay*.

41. Mrs. Strachey, in M. Goldsmith, *Women at War*, p.146.

42. Liverpool Civil Defence Emergency Committee *Minutes*, 25 October 1940.

43. Liverpool Education Committee *Minutes*, 10 October 1940.

44. M. Goldsmith, *Women at War*, p.156.

45. Board of Education White Paper, *Education Reconsidered*, July 1943, paragraph 25, p.8.

46. Ministry of Education, Circular 75, *Nursery Provision for Children under Five*, 14 December 1945.

47. Education Committee *Minutes*, 14 November 1946.

48. Public Health Department, *Report on the Health of the City of Liverpool*, 1947.

49. Oral Evidence 7.

50. G. Williams, *Women at Work*, p.118.

51. M. Goldsmith, *Women at War*, p.48.

Daily life in wartime Liverpool

As the months stretched into years, the population gradually adapted to the routines of wartime life. Rationing was introduced early in the War and by November 1941 covered a wide range of goods. As the war continued the list of rationed articles grew; soap became precious, chocolate treats were increasingly kept for special occasions and thickly buttered toast became a thing of the past. People were forced to restructure their eating habits in line with what was available. Dried eggs and fish were two of the more common food items recalled with horror. Lord Wolton, Minister of Food, was concerned to ensure that food was of a nutritional level necessary for a healthy diet so the 'national loaf' was introduced and, in December 1941, the Vitamin Welfare Scheme for children was launched. Apart from actual rationing there were shortages in almost every other article imaginable. Ordinary cooking pans became almost impossible to procure and this was a particular problem during periods of air attack when being 'bombed out' meant the necessary replacement of many household commodities.

Shopping for what goods there were placed almost everybody on the same level. All women had to queue everywhere for everything. For women who worked shopping held particular problems, especially if they had registered for rationed goods at shops near their homes but not necessarily near their work places. Although the Government urged employers to allow time off for shopping, in practise this didn't happen very often and working women had to shop in their lunch hour or on Saturday afternoons. If they were fortunate, women could find a neighbour or relative to help out in this respect, but for many women, shopping continued to be one of the more arduous features of daily life throughout the period.

'Towards the end of the War, I went to work in a cafe in Old Hall Street and the men who worked at the Corn Exchange got me all sorts. There was a fruit market behind that supplied the ships and I got fresh fruit regular all the time I worked there. It was just as well because with working I often missed out—you had to be there when the stuff came in. One of the women would come running back home and tell the others to, 'Get up to Turners', or whatever because he'd got a crate of oranges or something. Of course, by the time they got up there the word had got round and the queue was a mile long. Being at work, I didn't stand a chance.'[1]

Another woman, ten years old when the War broke out, remembered:

'If we were out and we saw a queue, my mother used to tell us to get in it while one of us ran home to get her. Most times you wouldn't even know when you joined the queue, just what you were queuing for!' (laughing)[2]

The provision of free or cheap school meals and milk became a prominent area of social policy. In November 1941, the Daily Post reported that Mr. R.A. Butler, President of the Board of Education, had said:

'... If children can be kept warm in school and have a good meal, it will be much better than having to walk home several miles. Nowadays, when so many women are engaged on war work, children may be neglected at midday.'[3]

As the war proceeded it became normal for children to remain in school at lunch time and much of the stigma attached to receiving school meals was thereby lifted.

During the War, overall, the physical condition of children did improve although this was not always very visible. In Liverpool, the prevalence of scabies reached almost epidemic proportions as the number of children treated increased from 693 in 1938 to 11,329 in 1943.[4] Initially, this was fuelled by evacuation and mobilisation but later by overcrowding and the increasing shortages of soap, towels, bedding, underclothes and laundry facilities. Nevertheless, despite the widespread problem, great advances were made in other areas of disease prevention and child welfare. Because of fear of epidemic, seven million children were immunised against diptheria between 1940 and 1945 and this resulted in a sharp decline in the number of deaths from the disease.[5] Nutritional levels were, in some cases, improved by rationing and food shortages as more well-balanced if basic diets were consumed and evacuation raised official consciousness about the condition of much of the nation's population. School meals, free or cheap milk and vitamin supplements contributed to improve the physical well-being of children during the War. In other ways, however, the State was less caring.

Prior to the outbreak of War, Liverpool Education Committee had maintained sixteen evening Play Centres during the winter months, which were open from 5.00 p.m. to 7.00 p.m., two evenings a week; because of war conditions these were not re-opened in the winter of 1939. But, as the war progressed, there was mounting concern in the city about increasing juvenile delinquency which was often accompanied by school truancy. Most of these problems were blamed on lack of supervision. With fathers and mothers engaged on war work children 'ran wild' and older children missed school because they assumed domestic responsibilities. Whatever the reasons, there was a great increase in teenage crime during the period. In March 1941, the Liverpool Daily Post reported:

'... Detective Inspector Sullivan said that, since the war, crimes by juveniles of ages fourteen and under twenty-one had increased tremendously in Liverpool. These boys formed themselves into gangs and were a positive danger to the community in districts where they lived.
The Judge said 'These gangs are a common danger. They impose a most undesirable strain on the Police who have other things to do. It is high time steps were taken to put an end to this sort of thing.'[6]

This type of concern grew and it became increasingly apparent that something had to be done to alleviate the situation. In July 1941, the Board of Education sent out a circular on the subject:

'... To prevent delinquency among children it is not enough to secure regular attendance at school, but also in leisure time, particularly when so many are evacuated or when one or both parents may be engaged in war work and away from home for many of the hours when children are free from school. There is evidence that children are getting out of hand through lack of domestic care, before and after school.'[7]

43

In the autumn of 1941, Play Centre facilities were resumed to keep children '... usefully and healthily occupied from the closure of afternoon school until mothers who were engaged in war work were able to return to their homes.'[8] By July 1941, fifteen centres were in operation with an average total attendance of 2,291 boys and girls. They were open from 4.15 p.m. to 6.15 p.m., for children five to fourteen years.[9] To the same ends, schools remained open during the holidays. Much of the blame for the increase in incidents involving juveniles, was laid at the doors of their mothers. However, the problems for individual mums must have been immense. Goaded by Government propaganda and personal necessity, they were pushed into employment. The emphasis was very much on the needs of the State war machine and the needs and difficulties of maintaining normal family life became secondary in official eyes, although the same officials were quick to lay responsibility firmly on women's shoulders when problems of control became apparent. Occasionally, some sympathy and understanding of the pressures on women may be seen, as when some School Attendance Officers questioned the prosecution of mothers for failing to ensure children attended school: '... With their husbands in the Army, women with four or five children have to go to work because they are unable to manage on their allowances. When the mother is away from home, something is bound to go wrong.'[10] But, on the whole, little attention seems to have been given to the emotional stress and confusion the experience of war brought into the lives of young men and women in their most impressionable years, although this must have contributed to the increase in juvenile delinquency remarked upon at the time.

The problem of teenagers was only one of a number confronting the authorities during the period. Mounting concern was being expressed at the rise in illegitimate births and the increasing incidence of venereal disease reported in women. In Liverpool, illegitimate live births increased not only in number, but as a proportion of total live births in the city between 1939 and 1945. In 1945 more than ten per cent. of all the babies born in Liverpool illegitimate, but from then on numbers rapidly fell back.[11]

Moralists were very concerned, although it seems probable that the main reason for the rise in illegitimacy was the failure of illegitimate conceptions to be legalised by marriage because of the dislocations of war. During the war the number of legitimate births decreased which might indicate that children were being born illegitimate who in other circumstances would have been born within marriage.

It is possible also that increased sexual awareness might have contributed to the increase in illegitimacy rates. Because so many women left the isolation of their homes to work in industry alongside other women, shared experience might have widened their knowledge and sexual aspirations. This type of theory is very tentative and impossible to measure but certainly many more younger women were living away from home and away from neighbourhood social controls which may have been a relevant factor. It is possible too, that the impending separation of couples, perhaps forever given the uncertainties and dangers of war, played a part. As one woman told me:

'...You had to be wise to them. They'd tell you anything so you'd let them. One fella told me he was being posted to the Far East the next day and he had a feeling he wouldn't be coming back. I did feel sorry for him but my mam would have killed me so I wouldn't, though I felt guilty for ages after. Later I found out he was married to a girl in Anfield and got not much further east of here than Manchester. They could tell a good tale, you had to be three steps ahead.'[12]

Whatever the causes, illegitimacy couldn't be ignored. Before the war, welfare provision for unmarried mothers and their children was very poor and the wartime situation made the inadequacies even clearer. Most of the help available, other than through the poor law institutions which many women were pushed into, was through voluntary agencies. These were generally run by religious bodies and/or adoption agencies who were keen to obtain infants for married couples who were unable to have their own. Attitudes were often very moralistic and some of the homes were run almost like houses of correction. As late as 1965 at least, one home in the North West still insisted that mothers who stayed there all wore the same grey uniforms.[13] The countrywide increase in illegitimacy forced the authorities into a reconsideration of the position of unmarried mothers and their children in society. Calder states: '...Unmarried mothers of the war years were of a 'new type' which amazed social workers to whom they were referred. They shunned the preachifying moral welfare centres and resented the primitive attitude of some of the voluntary homes.'[14]

In January 1944, the Minister of Health sent out a circular which called attention to the circumstances of illegitimate births which had been greatly increased by the state of war. He asked for the problem to be given 'earnest consideration' and felt the most promising line of attack to be the co-operation of welfare authorities with existing moral welfare associations and, where necessary, the re-inforcement of their work.[15] The Medical Officer of Health in Liverpool responded by announcing that a register of illegitimate children would be drawn up in which 'certain relevant facts will be recorded.'[16] He considered the main requirements for reconstruction and re-inforcing work were to have more Health Visitors specially trained in the subject and to provide foster mothers whose pay was guaranteed by the local authority which would assess the amount of the mother's contribution. He believed it was also necessary to provide additional homes of different types; clearing houses for mothers and babies until suitable arrangements could be made; temporary accommodation for babies awaiting adoption and homes for mothers and children to provide care for children while permitting mothers to go out to work—so keeping mothers and infants together.[17] These plans were obviously well thought out and, perhaps, well intentioned but they ultimately came to nothing. The Medical Officer of Health himself stated '... Most of these suggestions are not practicable at the present time—but long term policy may include them when the means are available.[18] The only practical help given to unmarried mothers by the Liverpool authorities in practice was to make additional grants to the voluntary organisations for the expansion of work not undertaken by the local authority and these grants were really only token gestures.[19]

After the war, the care of unmarried mothers remained primarily the concern of the adoption agencies who had little interest in providing accommodation which would enable mothers and babies to remain together. But the war meant that the local authorities could no longer ignore the needs of unmarried mothers and their children.

Yet another major source of worry to the health authorities and those concerned about the moral welfare of the population, during the war years, was the increasing incidence of venereal disease reported, particularly among women. At the time it was believed that the figures were evidence of increased promiscuity among women, and indeed, there may have been some truth in this. As noted above, contact with other women may have brought increased sexual awareness and knowledge. In June 1943 Mass Observation reported that:

'... Most of the local girls preferred to spend their time with Naval Ratings rather than civilians or members of the other services. The alliance between local girls and seamen is all the more important owing to the gradual increase in V.D. among the latter.'[20]

The same report went on to conclude that girls in Liverpool pubs were, on the whole, much younger than in other areas surveyed and that also there was a high degree of promiscuity in these pubs. It stated that Naval Ratings were popular because they had more money to spend on leave than members of the other Services or civilians and Naval Ratings had adopted the pub as a sexual market.[21] Perhaps this report is, though, not a particularly well balanced one. The pubs named in the survey were situated in the dockland area of the city centre where prostitution was more likely to be found. But, the Report does also indicate a possible reason for increased venereal disease among women, that the authorities appear to have given little attention to. Venereal disease was increasing among all servicemen. Many thousands of men had been mobilised and were shifting around the country from place to place. It may indeed by true that the startling increase in venereal disease among women was because of their increased promiscuity. But it seems probable that some women, who already formed part of stable relationships with one man, may have become infected because of his infidelity and promiscuity when away from home. Without more research, possible causes of increased venereal disease among women in the period 1939 to 1945 must remain tentative and inconclusive.

In any case, the vast majority of Liverpool women remained unaffected. Whilst concern expressed by the authorities was sometimes reflected in parents attitudes to their daughters behaviour, it is clear that most of the apparent reckless disregard of convention and reputation on the part of younger women, was merely a sense of fun and adventure rather than an indication of moral degeneration.

'... I used to get murdered, 'I'll teach you (smack) to walk (smack) out with sailors (smack, smack)'. You'd think we were on the streets at least (laughing). We weren't soft, we just wanted some fun and a good time. There was no more than that to it.'[22]

And again:

'... The G.I's would send yellow cabs to the factory to pick us up when we finished work. We'd all pile in and up to Burtonwood ... We'd have a dance and a laugh and then they'd send us back again, there was nothing more to it ... My father used to batter me with shoes, always the shoes, when I got in, not that it stopped me going again! (laughing)[23]

All the concern about the moral welfare of women, did not, however extend to the way in which women were regarded. Attitudes to women contained obvious contradictions.

Throughout the war the government urged women to keep up their appearance, both for their own morale but, more importantly, for their men's. Despite the influx of women into the rather unromantic world of industrial life, they continued to be regarded as sex symbols. In September 1943, a 'Hello Beautiful' competition was announced by the Walton Times, to find 'Bootle's Woman at War', with a first prize of three guineas (£3.15):

'... More than ever today the women of England have turned from the hearth to the factory, from making homes to making war ... we find beauty no longer in pleasure resorts but in Munitions Factories, the Armed Forces, the Land Army, etc.'[24]

Keeping 'young and beautiful' as the popular song exhorted was not easy during the war. Cosmetics were difficult to get as they were subjected to very detailed manufacturing regulations and were expensive even when available. Shadow economy marketing in cosmetics was widespread but improvisation was the main order of the day. Women dusted bicarbonate of soda under their arms to counteract perspiration, but not all the substitutes were quite so simple as this. Some, made with lead bases were actually dangerous and manufactured by confidence tricksters to exploit the shortages in the name of profit, but the side effects of others were sometimes the source of much hilarity:

'... Stockings were like gold so we took to doing our legs with leg tan and we'd take turns to draw in each others 'seams'. The only thing was, though, the colour was smashing in the house but it changed the longer we had it on and our legs would go bright orange. One night me and my sister did our hair with this henna stuff—we were meeting two chaps at the Pavvy. Anyway, when we got off the tram it was teaming and we got wet crossing over, you should have seen the fellers faces—the rain had made the dye run and we had orangey streaks all down our faces mixing with black where the burn't cork we'd used as mascara had run as well. We must have looked a sight—we didn't half laugh about it in work the next day.'[25]

Rationing affected more than just stockings. Fashion was very difficult in the midst of wartime austerities. Trousers, worn for leisure before the war, became accepted dress for all walks of life. They were practical and comfortable to work in and ideal when having to dress in a hurry following alarms. Lower heeled shoes became essential when having to walk home or get to a shelter quickly and 'turbans' were worn by everybody. The media often made a virtue of necessity as seen in this newspaper article giving advice to women on how to make the best of themselves:

'... Make-up is only the finishing touch to beauty. Health is vital to beauty—plenty of sleep, good posture, vegetable and salad foods to provide vitamins, and clean teeth (use kitchen salt). Five minutes a night spent brushing your hair is better than expensive shampoos and brilliantine ... war economy in clothes is a blessing to women ... no extra frills, simplicity is ultra chic. Clothing regulations are an incentive to the ingenuity of women.'[26]

Ingenuity was the key word. Tailoresses did good business in 'remodelling' pre-war clothes, but for many working class women there was nothing new in 'making do'. The austerity of the war years could have been no worse, and was in some cases even better, than the conditions that existed for the mass of the working class of Liverpool through the 1920's and 1930's. Depression and unemployment had conspired to ensure that one of the least of most women's problems was 'being in fashion', so in this respect, as with queuing and shopping, war was a great leveller.

Leisure habits were altered by the war, in many cases irreversibly. It became common for women to spend their free time in pubs, whereas in pre-war days, 'nice' girls were not seen in them. For many women though, the dual burden of industrial work and home work meant less time and opportunity for leisure pursuits. In 1940, when air raids were still disrupting 'normal' life, Mass Observation made an enquiry into women's leisure habits:

No. 9 *Josie May who joined the WRENS expecting to go to sea, but was sent to a cook-house in Scotland where she peeled hundreds of tons of potatoes until bunions released her from service.*

'...New responsibilities, new conditions, require a new self-sufficiency in ordinary women...In the stress and difficulty of aerial warfare, women stick to habit as far as circumstances allowed...cinema appears the most ingrained habit and has been found the last to go of outside leisure activities...it is a pleasant habit, it takes a woman away from herself which, in the midst of tension and disorder, is probably her greatest need.'[27]

Mass Observation found that women were increasingly spending their spare time in passive pursuits—cinema, knitting, listening to the radio, or, the most passive of all, 'doing nothing'. The report concluded:

'...Raids, lack of sleep, nervousness are the final challenge to leisure habits. In wartime, women tend to do what they have to do when they get the chance and increasingly to do nothing when they are not compelled to work, prepare to shelter, look after their family. There is a vicious circle leading to inactivity, talking, worrying.'[28]

It is important to remember though, that even before the war leisure for most of the women of dockland Liverpool had seldom been an integral part of everyday life. Very often caring for large families, in appalling housing conditions whilst trying to keep body and soul together on inadequate incomes, left most women very little time for 'leisure pursuits' passive or otherwise!

Nevertheless, the more active of the female community found plenty of escapes in the dance halls and clubs of the city from the boredom and monotony of everyday life. Daily life was made even more tolerable for many once the 'Yanks' landed. With the entry of America into the War, the G.I's became a common sight in Liverpool. By British standards, they had a seemingly endless supply of money, food, candy and stockings. Resented by British men, adored by children and admired by women, they quickly became part of the local scene. They were quick to flatter, generous and flamboyant and provided a welcome ego booster for women of all ages, although a woman who 'walked out' with an American G.I. was still laying herself open to condemnation. Mothers feared for their daughters' reputations and often justifiably. It was said that in Burtonwood a roadside notice appeared: 'To all G.I.'s—please drive carefully, that child might be yours'.[29] If a G.I. was unwilling to admit responsibility, obtaining a paternity allowance was almost

No. 10 *Munitions workers enjoying some free time.*

impossible and the United States Army was always quick to send to another part of the country, any soldier accused of impropriety. However, some relationships established between Liverpool women and Americans did endure and after the war, G.I. brides left Liverpool to begin new lives in America. Many more women who remained in the city, have fond memories of the Yanks:

> '...I was manageress in Wood's Cafe in London Road and we got a lot of Yanks and a lot of prostitutes in first thing after being on Lime Street all night. The Yanks would take the iron gates off for me and the girls bring in the milk churns. It was nothing to get a £2 tip from the Yanks. I was loaded when I worked there.'[30]

It is clear that Liverpool women have very mixed memories of the war years, living through that time has left an indelibile mark upon them that the years in-between have served only to re-inforce.

FOOTNOTES

1. Oral evidence 7.
2. Oral evidence 14, June 1986.
3. *Liverpool Daily Post*, 'More Children to Get Dinner at School', 4 November 1941.
4. Liverpool Education Committee, *Annual Reports on the School Medical Service*, 1938 and 1943.
5. R. Titmuss, *Problems of Social*, p.515.
6. *Liverpool Daily Post*, 'Boy Gangs of Liverpool', 6 March 1941.
7. Liverpool Education Committee *Minutes*, 10 July 1941.
8. Liverpool Education Committee *Minutes*, 8 October 1941.
9. Liverpool Education Committee *Minutes*, 8 October 1941.
10. *Walton Times*, 'School Attendance Officers', 2 February 1945.
11. Public Health Department, *Reports on the Health of the City of Liverpool, 1939-1945*.
12. Oral evidence 9.
13. Oral evidence 15, Woman, December 1967.
14. A. Calder, *The People's War*, p.400.
15. Public Health Department, *Circular No. 2866, Care of Illegitimate Children*, January 1944.
16. Maternity and Child Welfare Sub-Committee *Minutes*, 14 January 1944.
17. Maternity and Child Welfare *Minutes*, 14 January 1944.
18. Maternity and Child Welfare *Minutes*, 14 January 1944.
19. Maternity and Child Welfare *Minutes*, 14 January 1944.
20. Mass Observation, *Report No. 1836, Behaviour of Women in Liverpool Pubs*, June 1943.
21. Mass Observation, *Report No.1836*.
22. Oral evidence 9.
23. Oral evidence 5.
24. *Walton Times*, 'Bootle's Woman at War', September 1943.

25. Oral evidence 4.

26. *Walton Times*, 'Bootle's Woman', September 1943.

27. Mass Observation *Report No.290*.

28. Mass Observation *Report No.290*.

29. N. Longmate, *The G.I.'s*, London 1975, p285.

30. Oral evidence 10.

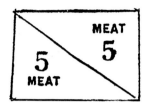

The war years considered

Retrospectively, it might be easy to conclude that the women who lived in Britain during the years 1939 - 1945, were the victims of a confidence trick on a massive and well organised scale. Their economic need and their patriotism were exploited by men in positions of power; by the Government, the trade unions, by private employers and by a nation anxious to win a war but not prepared to facilitate the involvement of women by the provision of equal wages or adequate facilities.

Necessity forced the recognition that it is physically impossible for women to give themselves wholeheartedly to industrial production if nothing is done to ease their burden of domestic labour. Nursery provision was made piecemeal, never met demands for it and was rapidly revoked once the War ended. Many women offered themselves as willing, unpaid handmaidens of the State which used their traditional 'talents' and 'skills' to re-inforce the British war machine.

Despite their role in the war effort, in industry and in social aid, images of women remained unchanged. They continued to be regarded by most men and largely by women themselves, as sexual objects and/or as maternal homemakers, only now these two roles had to be combined with some Britannia-like quality of productive industrial fervour. At all levels traditional values persisted despite the lip service paid to the problems of women within wartime society.

However, there were some positive aspects to the wartime experience of women. Perhaps the most important of these was the irreversible acceptance of part-time working as a feasible feature of factory employment. Another crucial change, which came directly out of the war, was the ending of the 'marriage bar'. The necessity of employing married women had proved they could be as responsible and reliable as those who were single.

Many of the progressive things that came out of the War were more an acceleration of pre-war trends than any complete re-appraisal of women in general. It has been estimated that if there had been no war there would have been about six and three quarter million women employed in 1943. The official estimate of women employed was seven and a half million so the '... trend was only hastened to the extent of about three-quarters of a million women.'[1]

Throughout the Inter-war period, the new fine-work, mass production industries of electrical engineering and confectionery had found a relatively cheap workforce in women and trade union membership was gradually increasing. But during the War more trade unions accepted women into their ranks for the first time and in some industries, even if partly motivated by elements of self-interest, male trade unionists had endeavoured to ensure women got the 'rate for the job'. However, even though the total number of women in trade unions had nearly doubled by 1943 to 1,870,000, with seven million women in the workforce, this still 'left a wide margin of non-unionised women'.[2] Also, membership of a trade union does not necessarily imply active participation.

The extension in the scope of employment into unfamiliar areas 'modified conventional ideas of what constituted women's work',[3] and made it more acceptable for women to be employed in areas outside their traditional occupations. But it is important not to over-exaggerate this trend. For most women their position post-1945 remained, in terms of employment, very much the same as it was pre-war. As Hopkins states:

> '... If a quarter of the nation's doctors were now women these were, in practice, mainly concerned with women's and children's diseases. If thousands of women worked in banks, the first woman bank manager (i.e. of a branch of a clearing bank) was appointed only in 1958. If there were 400 women in the Administrative Class of the Civil Service, they could claim only one Permanent Secretary and a couple of Deputy Secretaries ... In Industry, England ... was

still far from realising 'equal pay for equal work'. Anyhow, in practice work relatively rarely was equal. The traditional division of labour between men and women, broken by the urgencies of war, had quickly reasserted itself and women once again did the dull, repetitive jobs ... Their national average wage was about half that of men's.'[4]

Perhaps the last words should be those of a woman who lived through the war years:

'I don't really know if I can separate out the bits that I am because of the War from the person I would have been in any case. I think about it more now as I'm getting older; there was a feeling that you were part of things, I suppose I expected that to last but it didn't. It was a terrible, terrible time but there were good bits as well ... and, you know, I've thought since ... that women everywhere, on both sides, were having the same sorts of feelings ... that's the really sad part.'[5]

FOOTNOTES

1. **A. Calder,** *The People's War.*
2. P. Summerfield, Women Workers in the Second World War. *Capital and Class*, No.1, 1977.
3. G. Williams, *Women and Work*, p.96.
4. H. Hopkins, *The New Look*, London 1963, p.332.
5. Oral evidence 16. Woman, December 1986.

Suggested further reading

R. Broad and R. Fleming (eds.), *Nella Last's War : A Mother's Diary 1939-45*, Bristol, 1981.

A. Calder, *The People's War, Britain 1939-45*, London, 1971.

A. Johnson and K. Moore, *The Tapestry Makers - Life and Work at Lee's Tapestry Works, Birkenhead*, Liverpool 1987.

I. Law and J. Henfrey, *A History of Race and Racism in Liverpool, 1660-1950,* Liverpool 1981.

N. Longmate, *The G.I's,* London, 1975.

Second Chance to Learn Women's History Group, *Domestic Service in Liverpool 1850-1950,* Liverpool 1986.

M. Spring Rice, *Working Class Wives,* reprint, London, 1981.

Penny Summerfield, *Women Workers in the Second World War; production and patriachy in conflict,* London, 1984.